First Questions and Answers about **Animals**

TIME LIFE *for* Children®

ALEXANDRIA, VIRGINIA

Contents

Why don't animals wear clothes?

Because they don't have to! You wear clothes to protect your body from the weather. Animals have fur or feathers or scales or shells to cover them.

Animals stay warm in different ways. Dogs and cats have thick fur that keeps out the cold. Birds fluff up their feathers. This holds warm air close to their bodies.

Do wild animals live near my house?

A wild animal is an animal that has not been tamed or trained by people. It lives wherever it can find food and a safe home. That's why many wild animals live in towns, and even in cities. Look closely and you may see some near your home.

Why is that rabbit running away?

Wild animals have different ways of staying safe. Many animals run and hide when a larger animal comes near because they're afraid the bigger animal will hurt them. To a rabbit or a chipmunk, you look like a big scary animal. That's why the animal runs away when it sees you.

Did you know?
When a rabbit runs away, it does not go in a straight line. Instead, it hops in a zigzag path that makes the rabbit hard to catch.

Never try to catch or touch a wild creature, no matter how cute it looks. The same goes for pets you don't know.

Why does an opossum play dead?

Some animals use tricks to stay safe. When an opossum is in danger from a bigger animal, it pretends to be dead. The opossum falls over and lies still, hardly breathing at all. Even if the bigger animal sniffs it, the opossum doesn't move. That makes the bigger animal think the opossum is dead, so it leaves. After a while, the opossum gets up and goes on its way.

Did you know?

Other animals play dead, too.
When a hognose snake is in danger,
it rolls over and plays dead.
If another animal turns it over, the
snake will roll upside down again!

Try it!

When someone lies still without
moving, it's called "playing possum."
Can you play possum?

Do skunks stink?

No, but their spray does. When a skunk is cornered by another animal or a person, it sends a warning by stamping its front feet. It may also arch its back, the way a cat does, and make a hissing noise. If this does not scare away the animal or person, the skunk turns around, raises its tail, and squirts out a spray. The spray stings the eyes. It also smells so bad that the animal or person runs away—fast!

Did you know? One turtle lived to be 152 years old!

Why do turtles have shells?

Turtles are slow-moving animals, and most of them are very gentle. When scared, a turtle does not fight or run. Instead, it pulls its head, legs, and tail inside its shell. The shell is so hard that other animals cannot hurt the turtle as long as it stays inside.

Do all birds fly?

Birds need very strong muscles and big wings to fly. But some birds' wings are not big enough to lift their bodies off the ground. These birds can do other things very well, though. Penguins use their wings as paddles to swim underwater. And an ostrich runs faster than a person can pedal a bike.

Can other animals fly?

Yes! Birds aren't the only ones that can flap their wings and fly. Many insects can fly. So can bats, which catch and eat flying insects. If a bug gets caught in a bat's wing or tail, the bat scoops the bug into its mouth in midair!

Did you know?

Some animals don't fly like birds and bats, but they can still move through the air. Flying fish skim just above the ocean waves. A flying squirrel glides from tree to tree, using its flaps of skin like parachutes.

Are birds the only animals that lay eggs?

No, many animals lay eggs. Snakes, turtles, frogs, toads, fish, and lizards all lay eggs. So do spiders, and insects like butterflies and mosquitoes. Eggs come in all shapes and sizes. A fish egg is smaller than a drop of water, but an ostrich egg is bigger than a softball!

Are snakes slimy?

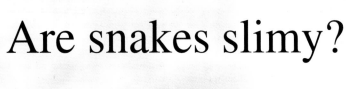

No, they just look that way. The skin of a snake is made of solid scales. These make it easy for the snake to slide over the ground. The scales are shiny, so the snake looks slimy, but really its skin is smooth and dry.

Did you know?

Snakes shed their skin when they grow too big for it, just like you take off a pair of pants. A young snake may shed its skin seven times in one year!

Why do monkeys have tails?

When a monkey swings through a tree, it uses its tail to keep its balance. Some monkeys can also use their tails as a "fifth hand" that holds on to branches. These monkeys can even hang upside down by their tails. This leaves their hands free to find food.

Did you know?
The tail of the red spider monkey is longer than its body. The red spider monkey can use its tail to pick things up!

25

How do other animals use their tails?

Horses chase away insects with their tails.

Fish and **whales** use their tails to swim through the water.

A tail comes in handy in many ways!

The beautiful tail feathers of a male **peacock** attract female birds.

A **beaver** smacks its flat tail on the water when danger is near.

A **kangaroo** uses its tail to keep its balance when it hops. Sometimes the kangaroo hops more than 40 feet!

Why does a kangaroo have a pocket?

The pocket is a pouch that helps a mother care for her baby. When a baby kangaroo is born, it climbs into the pouch and stays inside, drinking milk from its mother and growing. When it gets bigger, the baby climbs out. It spends more and more time out of the pouch, but it still goes back for a ride or a drink of milk!

What is the smallest animal?

Some animals are too tiny to see. But here are some of the smallest animals that you *can* see:

The **hognose bat** is so tiny that it weighs less than a feather.

The **bee hummingbird** is shorter than your finger. No bird is smaller than that!

The **pygmy marmoset** is the smallest monkey.

The world's littlest wild cat is called the **rusty-spotted cat.** It weighs less than three apples.

The **mouse deer** could be held in a grownup's hand.

The littlest snake is the **thread snake.** Can you see why that's a good name?

Did you know?

Many big animals start out very small. A panda weighs only about as much as a birthday card when it is born. But by the time it is fully grown, it is heavier than a football player!

31

What's the largest animal?

The **elephant** is the biggest animal that lives on land. It can weigh almost eight tons. That's more than a dump truck!

A **giraffe** is taller than any other animal. The biggest giraffe ever measured was higher than a house!

Did you know?
A blue whale is much bigger than the largest dinosaur that ever lived.

The **blue whale** is the largest animal in the world. It can weigh more than a train locomotive!

The largest turtle, the **Pacific leatherback,** grows to be as long as a surfboard.

33

How does an elephant use its trunk?

An elephant's trunk helps the elephant eat. The elephant grabs food with its trunk and puts it in its mouth.

The trunk lets the elephant drink. A thirsty elephant sucks water into its trunk like a straw. Then it squirts the water into its mouth.

The trunk lets the elephant take a bath.
When the animal gets hot, it sprays
water on its head and back. It also
likes to cover itself with dust or mud;
this keeps bugs from biting.

Why are giraffes so tall?

A giraffe uses its long neck to reach its food—the tasty leaves that grow near the tops of tall trees. Being tall helps in other ways, too. A giraffe can spot dangerous animals just by looking around.

Did you know?

A giraffe's neck is not long enough to reach the ground! To get a drink of water, the giraffe must spread its legs or bend its knees.

Why can't I pet a lion?

A lion in a zoo may look tame, but you can't go near it or pet it because it is a dangerous wild animal. It has sharp claws and teeth that could really hurt you. The lion isn't bad—it's just a natural hunter.

Wild animals are very different from the animals we keep as pets. Most dogs and cats are used to people, but wild animals are not. That's why it's important to leave wild animals alone.

Why do tigers have stripes?

Tigers live in jungles or tall grass, where their stripes make them hard to see. That's how a tiger can sneak up on another animal and catch it for dinner.

40

Did you know?
No two tigers are striped the same way. It's easy for them to tell each other apart.

Why are pandas black and white?

No one really knows! Some people think the black and white marks protect a panda by making it hard to see in the snow. Other people think the marks are a warning sign, like the stripes on a skunk. To another animal, the black and white marks on a panda could mean, "Back off—I bite!"

Did you know?

A panda spends most of its time eating juicy bamboo shoots. If you were a wild panda, you would eat bamboo all day long!

43

Do bears give bear hugs?

Not unless you're a bear, too! Bears are too big, too strong, and too wild to hug people.

Sometimes a bear shakes its head from side to side when it sees another bear. That's the bear's way of saying, "Do you want to play with me?" Then the two animals stand on their back legs, grab each other with their arms, and push. It looks like they're giving each other a big hug!

That reminds me of someone I want to hug. Let's head for home!

Do animals laugh?

Animals don't laugh or cry as we do, but you can still tell how they feel. When a dog wags its tail and licks your hands or face, you know it is happy to see you!

TIME-LIFE for CHILDREN®

Managing Editor: Patricia Daniels
Editorial Directors: Jean Burke Crawford, Allan Fallow,
                          Karin Kinney, Sara Mark, Elizabeth Ward
Editorial Coordinator: Marike van der Veen
Production Manager: Marlene Zack
Senior Copyeditor: Colette Stockum
Production: Celia Beattie
Supervisor of Quality Control: James King
Assistant Supervisor of Quality Control: Miriam Newton
Library: Louise D. Forstall, Anne Heising

Special Contributor: Barbara Klein
Researcher: Jocelyn Lindsay
Writer: Andrew Gutelle

Designed by: **David Bennett Books**

Series design: David Bennett
Book design: Andrew Crowson
Art direction: David Bennett & Andrew Crowson
Illustrated by: Tessa Richardson-Jones
Additional cover
 illustrations by: Nick Baxter

© 1994 Time Life Inc. All rights reserved.

First printing. Printed in U.S.A.   2/06
Published simultaneously in Canada.

Time Life Inc. is a wholly owned subsidiary of THE TIME INC. BOOK COMPANY.

TIME-LIFE is a trademark of Time Warner Inc. U.S.A.
For subscription information, call 1-800-621-7026.

Library of Congress Cataloging-in-Publication Data

Do bears give bear hugs? : first questions and answers about animals.
p. cm. — (Library of first questions and answers)
ISBN 0-7835-0870-0.
1. Animals—Miscellanea—Juvenile literature. [1. Animals—Miscellanea.
2. Questions and answers.] I. Time-Life for Children (Firm) II. Series.
QL49.D59 1994   93-44296
596—dc20   CIP
                                                                AC

Consultants

Dr. Lewis P. Lipsitt, an internationally recognized specialist on childhood
development, was the 1990 recipient of the Nicholas Hobbs Award for science in
the service of children. He has served as the science director for the American
Psychological Association and is a professor of psychology and medical science at
Brown University.

Thomas D. Mullin directs the Hidden Oaks Nature Center in Fairfax County, Virginia,
where he coordinates workshops and seminars designed to promote appreciation for
wildlife and the environment. He is also the Washington representative for the
National Association for Interpretation, a professional organization for naturalists
involved in public education.

Dr. Judith A. Schickedanz, an authority on the education of preschool children, is
an associate professor of early childhood education at the Boston University School
of Education, where she also directs the Early Childhood Learning Laboratory. Her
published work includes *More Than the ABC's: Early Stages of Reading and Writing
Development* as well as several textbooks and many scholarly papers.